# EVE
## in overalls

### WOMEN AT WORK IN
### THE SECOND WORLD WAR

ARTHUR WAUTERS

First published c.1942

First published in this format in 2017 by IWM,
Lambeth Road, London, SE1 6HZ
iwm.org.uk

© The Trustees of the Imperial War Museum, 2017

ISBN 978-1-904897-35-4

A catalogue record for this book is available from the British Library
Printed and bound in the UK by Gomer Press

Front cover image: Laura Knight, *Ruby Loftus Screwing
a Breech-ring*, 1943. Oil on canvas. IWM ART LD 2850
Back cover image: Cosmo Clark, *Women Required for Motor
Driving and Telephonist Duties*, 1941. Poster. IWM PST 3673
Illustrations (redrawn from the original publication) on
pages 2, 12, 18, 24, 32: © Peter Collins
Pic credits: © British Official Photo/Getty Images: page 40;
© Mirrorpix: page 7 (right); page 39 (right)

FSC
www.fsc.org
MIX
Paper from
responsible sources
FSC® C114687

# CONTENTS

# INTRODUCTION

The Second World War generated a colossal demand for labour. It was a 'total war' in every respect, and the civilian population of Britain was involved in the fight as it had never been before. As men were drafted into the armed services, vacant jobs needed to be filled to keep the country running. At the same time, increased production for the war effort was vital if Britain was to have a hope of winning. The government had to make the best possible use of all the resources at its disposal, and women stepped up to the task in their millions. They worked in a hugely diverse range of jobs, from pilots, engineers and manufacturers to air raid wardens, signallers, code breakers and secret agents.

First published during the Second World War, *Eve in Overalls* highlights the enormous contribution made by women, in an era when such progress was often overlooked. The style of language used is old-fashioned even for the time, and reflects the fact that women were entering what was very much seen as a man's world. Though the author praises women's 'tranquil heroism', the patronising tone may seem shocking to readers today.

The pamphlet is of course a product of its time, and the style reflects many attitudes of the 1940s. Women in the workplace were viewed with curiosity and fascination, as they were taking on roles that were traditionally thought to be unsuitable for them. Yet, as *Eve in Overalls* shows, women weren't afraid of getting their hands dirty — and they proved they were more than capable of rising to the challenge.

Before the outbreak of war in 1939, more women than men had started to volunteer for the brewing conflict. Voluntary work offered women a sense of freedom and adventure, an escape from the predictable path to motherhood and domesticity. The Women's Voluntary Service (WVS), established in 1938, provided over a million women to help ordinary families during the war.

The women organised the evacuation of children, collected salvage, knitted, sewed and raised money for warships, aeroplanes and tanks through the National Savings Movement. Many worked in the midst of the action in Air Raid Precautions (renamed Civil Defence in 1941). They ran mobile canteens, Citizens Advice Bureaux and Rest Centres during the Blitz. Thousands volunteered in the Women's Land Army (WLA) – more than 80,000 at its peak in 1944 – replacing agricultural workers who had gone to fight.

Though Ernest Bevin, Minister for Labour, realised that the employment of women would be essential to help Britain's war effort, he had hoped that their role would be 'limited'. However, with pressure mounting on the labour market, by the end of 1941 he had no choice but to introduce – for the first time ever in British history – the compulsory conscription of single women. This was to have a major change on the lives of women across society.

Women were offered the choice of a role either within industry or in one of the services.

Thousands worked in the factories, producing essential war equipment from aircraft to munitions. It was sometimes back-breaking and often dangerous work. The toxic mix of chemicals and explosives in munitions factories caused several accidents where women were gassed. Yet the factories often fostered feelings of comradeship and togetherness, especially in times of danger or over unfair treatment of women by the management.

A role in one of the three services offered women the chance to learn new skills, to travel, and to undertake new responsibilities that previously had been closed to them.

With over 250,000 female personnel, the Auxiliary Territorial Service (ATS) was by far the largest of the women's services. While some duties included tasks such as cooking and clerical work, many women became ammunition inspectors and military police, and a large number operated anti-aircraft searchlight batteries.

The ATS was considered one of the less glamorous services, with the uniform derided as 'hideous' by popular novelist Barbara Cartland. Efforts were made to change this, with stylish recruitment posters featuring 'blond bombshells' adorning the streets. Later, these posters were banned for being too frivolous.

The service which many women aspired to join was the Women's Royal Naval Service (WRNS or 'Wrens'), though this was the smallest of the women's services, with just 74,000 serving by 1944. The Wrens played a major role in the planning and organisation of many of the Navy's operations. They were also a vital part of the smooth running of naval activities ashore.

Initially, joining the Wrens didn't mean a life in the midst of the action and, as women were discovering across the board, there was little enthusiasm for them to play a front line role. For many women joining the Wrens the reality was either a clerical role or a position as store assistant, driver or cook. Nevertheless, as the war progressed, women were given greater opportunities, and they could gain qualifications in meteorology, communications and radar.

Many women became signallers, releasing male signallers for sea-going duties. They worked on wireless telegraphy, visual signalling and coding. Though the majority remained in roles on shore, some women served at sea as members of boat crews. On a lighter note, the stylish navy blue uniform was generally considered to be the most attractive of all the services, in part adding to the appeal of joining the Wrens.

The third service, the Women's Auxiliary Air Force (WAAF), also opened up more and more opportunities for women as the war went on, and it came to be viewed as one of the more progressive and 'modern' services. Though initially only recruited to fill posts such as clerks, kitchen orderlies and drivers, women could later become mechanics, engineers, electricians and fitters for aeroplanes. They operated balloon barrages, interpreted aerial photographs, and intercepted codes and ciphers – including at the Government Code and Cypher School at Bletchley Park.

Many members of the WAAF worked on the radar control system as mechanics and operators, carrying out essential work during the Battle of Britain. Yet one job that was not open to the women of the WAAF was that of flying aircraft on the front line. Although women trained as pilots in secondary roles, to release their male counterparts for active service, the RAF thought it unacceptable to have women flying in a military capacity. Their role was limited to the home front, providing essential services in the Air Transport Auxiliary - from delivering new aeroplanes from factories to the often dangerous job of shuttling damaged aircraft back for repairs.

Images of women in the Second World War as land girls, nurses and housewives are familiar to us today, popularised in part through books and films such as *Land Girls*, *Mrs Miniver*, *Atonement* and *Their Finest*. But, as *Eve in Overalls* shows, the work they carried out involved an enormous number of lesser known and unexpected jobs. They ran ARP posts and drove ambulances. They worked as 'Lumber Jills' in the Women's Timber Corps, and a small number became secret agents in the Special Operations Executive (SOE), dropping into enemy territory and working as saboteurs, couriers and radio operators. They worked on the railways, canals and on buses. Today's Waterloo Bridge in London was mostly built by women during the Second World War. Women had challenged the inequality myth by proving that they could work just as hard as men.

In total, over 10 million women played their part helping Britain win the war. Of these, over 700 women working in the ATS, WRNS, WAAF and the forces nursing services died for their country.

The opportunities that opened up to women through work in the Second World War were, for many, hugely liberating. Some were propelled to lives unimaginable before the outbreak of war, freeing them from the confines of family or rural life to exciting and challenging new possibilities.

At the war's end, however, women were not considered equal to men. Throughout the war men continued to be paid more than women who were doing the same jobs. It was generally considered that the women were just temporarily filling in for the men, while they were away fighting. When the war ended it was expected by many that women should dutifully return to the home (though it should be added that this expectation was also held by many women themselves). By 1951 the number of women in paid employment had dropped to just below the pre-war level.

However, the opportunities and experiences that women gained through their work in the Second World War gave them a confidence that they could do it. They had proved to themselves, if to no one else, that they were equally as competent as men. They had helped win the war and, as *Eve in Overalls* affirms, 'Great Britain, defending her freedom, has contracted an immense debt of gratitude to the women'.

IWM curatorial team

# EVE
## in overalls
### by Arthur Wauters

# EVE

# in khaki

LITTLE MORE than forty years ago the occupations open to women could be counted on the fingers. For centuries women have worked on the land, and there were also housekeepers, dressmakers, milliners, governesses, secretaries, nurses, shop assistants, mill-girls, waitresses, etc. The first woman lawyer, however, caused a great sensation, the first woman doctor almost started a riot, and the first policewoman was looked upon as a personal affront by the stronger sex.

Since then men have had to suffer many defeats in the labour market. Women have invaded every sphere. There is hardly any kind of work left where they have not succeeded in taking the place of men. This phenomenon has grown with startling rapidity, especially during the present War. It has provoked a veritable

*A.T.S. are in the front line in Britain to-day, operating searchlights and gun-sights. This identification telescope picks up hostile aircraft, giving bearing and angle of sight.*

*Two W.R.N.S. training to be Wireless Telegraphists at a Naval Establishment, where morse is automatically written on tapes at 200 to 300 words a minute.*

psychological and social revolution. Woman has completely lost her inferiority complex. Technical developments and improvements, by removing or considerably reducing all physical effort, have made it possible for women to enter any and every profession. It is even possible for them now to take up occupations from which they were previously barred, because the work was too hard, too dangerous or too unhealthy. They are quite at their ease doing these jobs, and look at their male colleagues with sly impudence.

For all the belligerents without exception, the problem of industrial labour has become infinitely more acute than that of military effectives.

It is generally agreed that it requires seven workmen to feed, equip and transport one soldier. When the American troops landed in

Northern Ireland, it was said that each combatant brought five tons of material with him. These figures give some idea of the extent of the effort made by the peoples who wish to remain free.

To judge by the effort being made in Great Britain, the British certainly will remain free.

Women have not only entered factories by the million, but they are taking a direct and increasing share in actual defensive military operations. They are doing so either as volunteers or by compulsion as a result of the law which draws them into the service of the nation as conscripts. This surprising event took place in a country which knew nothing of military conscription, and where individual liberty had achieved a degree unknown in any other region of the world, and each time that the Government increased its compulsory measures, they were unanimously approved by public opinion. In the by-elections which have been held since the declaration of War, the Government has only been defeated by candidates who proposed to go even further as regards the total mobilisation of the energies of the nation; and these elections took place at a time when the Allies were suffering severe reverses.

*Postwomen are a familiar sight to-day, clearing pillar boxes and delivering letters all over the country.*

What work do these women do in the sea, land and air services?

First and foremost, they carry out jobs which do not necessarily require male collaboration. They act as orderlies, messengers, telephonists and secretaries. They work as cooks, bus-conductresses, and postwomen. They have naturally enough taken charge of canteens and shops. They are also playing an increasingly important role in transmission and liaison work. They have become extremely expert as signallers, they make admirable meteorologists and they fully appreciate the importance of secret messages. They repair the parachutes made by their comrades in the factories; they take photographs, they work as electricians and they make guns, and an ever-increasing number pilot aeroplanes from the factories to the aerodromes.

Women have taken the men's place in laboratories and it is they who handle the wireless sets. It is they, too, who test sparking plugs,

*Mary Begg, whose husband works in an aircraft factory, now sees the trains off at Euston Station.*

*Irene Wragg is a twenty-one-year-old employee of the London Midland and Scottish Railway and her job is to load the delivery vans with supplies sent by rail.*

*Mrs. Winzer and Mrs. Talbot work on a new job for women, cleaning tubes in the smoke box of a "Sandringham" class locomotive, on the London and North Eastern Railway.*

and they naturally have an important place in ambulance work. 1,300 of them accompanied the Army to France, Greece and Iceland. Quite a few have been decorated for acts of exceptional bravery.

Women are also trained in the fire services, the police and the organisations created to take care of air-raid victims.

They do all these jobs with remarkable courage and professional conscientiousness. After the bombs have fallen during an air raid, there are injuries to be treated, temporary lodgings to be found for those rendered homeless and who have to be moved and fed, and children to be evacuated.

During the night of May 10th, 1941 London had a particularly severe raid. At the place where I was at the time there were some casualties. The majority of them were not a pleasing sight. It must have required a great deal of strength of character to approach these mutilated limbs, these gaping heads and torn bodies. The women

7

*Most of the London buses now carry women conductresses. Here is one of them checking over the day's schedule with her driver at the depot.*

*This girl, checking an engine, is a maintenance worker in a London Passenger Transport Board garage. She helps to keep the London buses running, by replacing men mechanics who are called-up for military service.*

who were looking after them did so quietly and methodically without any sound or agitation or flurry, and above all without any fuss. Some of them offered their services spontaneously, although it was not part of their job. The following day I found them all back at their normal tasks. Their eyes looked tired and their faces were pale, but not one made any mention of the tragedy of the night before. This tranquil heroism is to be found wherever the women of Britain are calmly and quietly carrying out their civic duties.

Discretion does not allow the mention of many figures, but a few are available which make it possible to judge the value of women's contribution to the defence of endangered liberty.

There are 700,000 women enrolled in the Ministry of Health services alone. They look after maternity cases, crèches and homes for the evacuated, and it is they too who had to deal with the transfer to the country of over a million children of school age.

125,000 women are now on the Post Office staff, 2,000 of whom are doing work previously only undertaken by qualified craftsmen. They are now entrusted with the laying of telephone wires, their adjustment and other mechanical jobs.

*A volunteer "pick and shovel" gang trench-digging and laying a power cable at a Southern Railway depot.*

*A real man's job—but two women got down to shovelling coal dust on to a railway truck. Mrs. Makins has two children at school and her colleague, Mrs. Morris, is the mother of five grown-up children.*

*Women are now being trained to act as ground crews at Bomber and Fighter Stations, thus releasing men for other duties. At this Fighter Station, W.A.A.F.S. are shown refuelling a plane.*

In the realm of transport there are even more surprising things to be seen. There are, it need hardly be said, women station masters and ticket collectors. The Greater London underground network has one woman for every eight members of the staff. On the railways they act as porters, deal with luggage, and even drive the electric trolleys. They are responsible for the signals and signal boxes and they clean down the engines. And at the ports there are a number of women dockers to be found.

Have you ever painted the underneath of a bridge as it stretches over a river? I imagine not, but there are women doing it in Britain.

All these women are not necessarily working for payment. There is the Women's Voluntary Service with over a million members. They have all signed on for the duration of the War and their work is absolutely voluntary. The woman who drove me recently was a University woman who had specialised in ethnography. She was donating her time, her car, and her money to War work.

# BEAUTY

## and the blimps

A CAPTIVE BALLOON is not very war-like. First and foremost, it is a prisoner, and, to judge by its bad temper and impatience, it finds this very annoying.

When on the ground it makes one think of an elephant sorrowfully flapping its ears and sadly meditating on its conjugal misfortunes. When in the air, it resembles a rickety, anaemic, aerodynamic archangel awaiting some message from the skies. It is a truly Walt Disney creation.

But in spite of its laughable and ridiculous appearance, it is a very formidable defensive weapon. Its harmless and homesick mien is deceptive in the extreme.

The one I saw was lodged in the middle of a square in a large town. In the midst of debris from a recent raid, children were playing "catch" round it.

Its crew was composed entirely of women, all of whom were very young. Not very long ago their pretty hands must still have been playing with toy balloons. It cannot have been very long ago either since they were still engrossed with dolls. The balloon has increased in size, the toy has become this monstrous insect, tearing impatiently at its gigantic umbilical cord.

The care of a captive balloon is not what the uninitiated may think. It is a greedy animal. When it is brought down from the skies, it has to be given its bottle. Tractors, driven by young girls, bring huge jujubes filled with gas.

Then it has to be hoisted. The pull on its mooring ropes must be regulated in accordance with the velocity of the wind, the visibility and the hygrometric condition of the air. All this requires a

*Britain's Balloon Barrage defence is one of the toughest jobs that the W.A.A.F. have taken on. This airwoman, helping to bed down a balloon, wears the working aircrew suits and boots.*

13

considerable amount of dexterity, method, co-ordination and physical strength. The girls carry out all this work with strict military discipline, and it is all done with perfect good humour.

They are all radiantly healthy and warmly clad. At night when it is windy and wet, the temperature falls rapidly, but they are snugly wrapped in waterproof uniforms. By a curious phenomenon of professional mimicry, they themselves very much resemble miniature captive balloons. Yet feminine coquetry will never give up all its claims. Whether under a cap or a steel helmet, their hair—and this is generally very beautiful in England—is arranged to show the permanent waves to the very best advantage.

*This W.A.A.F. trainee is learning how to inflate a barrage balloon correctly.*

*An outsize ladder is used by the girls to attend to the fins as the balloon is being inflated.*

The number of members forming a balloon crew is considerable. There are thousands of stations in Great Britain of the same kind. There are 3,500 miles of coastline to be protected, apart from places of vital importance and industrial centres. A fair estimate of the number of men that have thus been freed for more dangerous jobs can easily be reckoned.

I noticed a horse-shoe over the doorway of the main billet. Houses with gaping walls, heaps of rubble on the ground, twisted rails and broken stone pillars showed, however, that the German Air Force has not had very much respect for this innocent faith in the superstition of a childish luck-bringer.

Here we are at Z.S. 13.

Z.S. 13 is the site of an anti-aircraft battery—somewhere in England. The sun is shining on the gentle slopes of the hills, a soft breeze is whispering among some of the loveliest trees in the world.

15

The view stretches away to the distant horizon that inspired the brush of Turner.

Quick-moving and alert-looking young women with frank and laughing eyes are busily occupied with complicated scientific instruments. They handle them with the ease and dexterity of an experienced optician. They identify enemy aircraft, determine their altitude and calculate with startling precision their probable course. They pass on this information in clear musical tones to the firing posts. They do all this very quickly, without the slightest trace of hesitation in their actions, which shows the very advanced degree of their training.

*W.A.A.F.S. not only have to look after their balloon, but they have to know how to make necessary repairs.*

*With the balloons safely tucked away in their hangars for the night, these girl operators march off duty at the end of a day's intensive training.*

They wear exactly the same uniform as their men comrades, but they have not lost any of the allure of their sex.

One of them asked me, with feigned anxiety:

"Don't you think that we are becoming a little too mannish?" She was very sure of the reply. She knew very well that there was no question of gallantry conflicting with truth, for she had magnificent eyes, lovely hair and a delightful mouth, and, what was more, she was well aware of this, and was even more aware that no one could long resist her bewitching smile.

But as I left them, I could not help wondering about the future of these young things, spending their time in the hubbub of camp life, sleeping in huts, living under the most complete community conditions, freed from all normal restraint. And I thought of my grandmother, a charming and tender wraith:

"Where, oh where, Grandmama, are your jars of preserves and your press full of scented linen?"

# PENELOPE

## mechanised

THE CAR IS pushing through the country. We are crossing England —proud, placid, devout, morose England. The fog is as opaque as solid concrete. The countryside is sallow and wan, like an overdose of absinthe.

Occasionally, a feeble ray of sunshine pierces the shroud. There then emerge what Jules Balles called with somewhat biased enmity "those rows of tombs." These are the English "corons," silent witnesses of an out-of-date mode of life of evil repute, the dismal tatters of an industrial civilisation justly loathed by Ruskin and William Morris. The pits devour the miners who take up this heroic, yet accursed trade.

One is nothing more here than one among other men . . .

*These girl drivers are expected to keep their vehicles in first-class running conditions so thorough training is given in maintenance as well as in driving.*

19

*These women are milling the jacket of a jim, vast numbers of which are being turned out at this factory.*

A little farther on, the proud outposts of apoplectic industry rise up, chimney stacks, overhead railways, bridges, docks, cranes, and factory after factory.

Aeroplanes are to be seen at every stage of the journey. They pass by unassembled, on fast-moving lorries. They drone overhead or swoop slowly down on to the landing grounds.

It is here that Great Britain, with the aid of the women, is forging her shield.

There is something desperate and tyrannical in this war of production. Men are in the grip of a sullen frenzy and wild passion. They are a prey to the craze for metal and fire. There is no place here for dreaming or fantasy or frivolity.

Life is spent in a brutal kind of wild delirium. The manufacture of war material is the star to be culled from the sky. Incandescent ingots steer wild orbits through the spark-filled air. Implacable stamps clasp and smother them. Vats and ladles pour molten metal into moulds as they move by in quivering columns on endless belts.

Compressed-air machines set up a shrill yelping. Acetylene blowpipes spit forth blinding comets of light. Forges, like witches' cauldrons, illumine the shop with weird lights. Pneumatic hammers stutter sharp moans. Steel and copper shavings cap the machine tools with permanent waves . . .

In the very midst of the dust and smoke and diabolical uproar thousands of women are working.

Through a slit in the workshop window I suddenly caught sight of a horse standing in the sunshine peacefully cropping bright green grass. This unexpected pastoral note came like an offensive joke.

At the time of the "Enclosures" sheep were kept at the expense of men. Horse-power is now doing away with the live horse.

A few rakes and ploughs lie abandoned in a dark corner, humble, despised relics of defunct peace . . .

This factory, which is producing nothing but guns—and I saw thousands there—consists of nine large parallel shops. Each one is 665 yards long and there are 3,000 women employed.

*Hundreds of thousands of women are working in Army clothing factories, either full-time or part-time, making battle dressed and other equipment for the troops.*

*Armament workers in a big Munitions Factory, handling lathes expertly.*

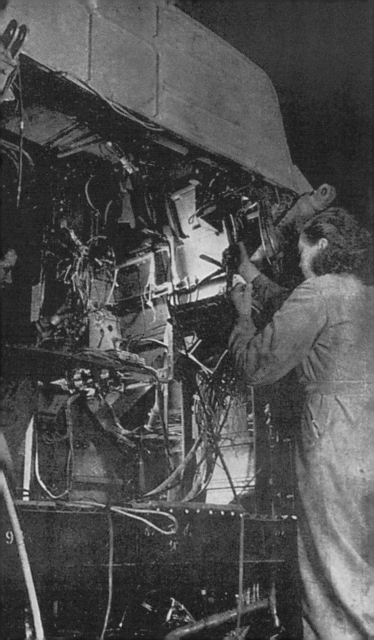

Aero factory girls learn how to dismantle damaged aircraft for salvage of parts.

From their raised positions the pack of travelling cranes joins the hunt for breech-blocks, ingots, engines, and with punctual and precise gesture, like so many great spiders, they seize on them as they pass and lay them down on the benches with courtly grace. Women are working these machines with careful precision, carrying out their tasks methodically, their faces betraying the strain and concentration.

One of them has a few moments' rest. She immediately begins to knit, to knit for the absent son or distant husband, away somewhere in Libya or the Far East.

Penelope mechanised . . .

Here is another. She is only eighteen years old. She is in sole charge of a machine tool worth £4,000. Her knowledge of machinery was previously limited no doubt to a bicycle or a sewing-machine. Not so long ago she was working in a cinema.

And here is another. Her grinder is polishing very complicated-looking pieces of steel. Her head is surrounded by a halo of sparks. She is humming Schubert's "Song of Love."

And this one, with her body bent forward, is using a paint sprayer. Paint spraying has always been looked at askance by medical and factory inspectors.

I felt as though I had been taking part in a great pagan feast . . .

# MODERN

# dairymaid

THE AGRICULTURAL PROBLEM in Great Britain is one of the most curious in Europe, and one of the most complicated.

The population of the United Kingdom has increased by nearly seven million since the last war, while the area under cultivation has decreased by several million acres. This was due to the spreading of the towns and the construction of aerodromes which, more often than not, encroach on to the most fertile soil. Great Britain depended on her neighbours and her Empire for a considerable portion of her food supplies. The Axis' military successes have not made the solution of this problem any easier.

*Joan Arden used to work in a Manchester solicitor's office, but now she works as a land girl helping her father on his farm at Swinton.*

Democratic Britain did not shrink from facing these difficulties. Democratic methods in practical application have achieved success, for democracy has crossed the political frontier and entered into the economic sector. We have already seen what has been done in industry. The same kind of thing is being done in agriculture. The Government is elaborating the principles of its agricultural policy in agreement with the associations of land-owners, farmers and agricultural labourers. Mixed committees, composed of an equal number of delegates from similar professional groups, are entrusted with the development of these ideas.

The results are surprising. The area under cultivation has increased since the war by six million acres. The quantity of corn grown alone has risen by a third, potatoes by 60 per cent, and sugar even more. At the present time four million tons of vegetables are produced, whereas in 1938 this figure was only two and a half million tons. And there are three million small private gardens, which supply between ten and fifteen million pounds' worth of vegetables every year.

Science has played a big part in these encouraging improvements. Agriculture in Great Britain is to-day the most mechanised in Europe. More tractors are used than in Germany, although a smaller area is under cultivation than in the Reich.

No mistake, however, must be made about the importance and effect of the introduction into agriculture of scientific processes; biological selection, cold and vacuum storage, artificial fertilisation, drainage and irrigation, the frost, pests and diseases—all these

*Kathleen Leach was a Court dressmaker before the war, but now she handles an 80 h.p. Diesel Caterpillar Tractor at a farm in Hertfordshire. Girls are tackling men's jobs on the land to-day and making a success of them too.*

26

*Two members of the Women's Land Army at work in the barn of a Hertfordshire farm.*

can to a considerable degree lessen the rigours of nature. But in agriculture machinery does not play nearly as important a part as in industry. For the latter it helps enormously to increase the output of goods for the market. This is not the case with agriculture. A machine can carry out certain work better and more quickly than can be done by hand, but the laws of germination and growth are immutable. Man has not yet succeeded in speeding up the rhythm.

The agricultural problem, therefore, still remains everywhere a problem of manual labour. No solution could have been reached here without the collaboration of women. It is to a large degree the fine army of land girls that has made it possible to win the battle of supplies in the British Isles.

Farmers were at first a little afraid—many on account of their crops and no doubt a few on account of their morals—of these women so pertly dressed up as men. A member of the House of Commons tried, however, to convince them by recalling that after all, from the beginning Eve had shown a great interest in the cultivation of fruit. He did not emphasise, it is true, the regrettable consequences of this first experiment, regrettable for the male sex and for humanity as a whole.

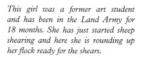

*On the left: Two new recruits to the Women's Land Army making friends with young calves at the Institute of Agriculture, at Usk in Monmouthshire.*

*This girl was a former art student and has been in the Land Army for 18 months. She has just started sheep shearing and here she is rounding up her flock ready for the shears.*

I have seen these women at work on the delightful farms of Kent, where the barns are thatched, romantic-looking barns, so cool in summer and so warm in winter. There are women of all types and ages among these land girls, though they are generally somewhere between 17 and 40, and all are volunteers. None of those to whom I have spoken had been connected in any way whatever with rural life before. They had previously been mannequins, manicurists, chorus girls, shop assistants, etc. I have never before been so struck by joy of living, suppleness of gait, vivacity and moral balance. They look gracefully gay in their riding breeches, and they are happy. The majority of them have only one desire: to continue their work on the farms after the war. Their health is excellent; their food is more varied and more abundant than in the towns. They have a variety of jobs to do, of far less monotonous character than in the factories—and out in the open air.

The town dweller who wanders through the fields in the spring is enraptured by the Virgilian life of the country people. The corn, as soft as down, is caressed by the breeze and stirs under the gentle rays of the sun. Apple trees are clothed in princely garb. The English countryside takes on a chaste and luminous mien. Spring has incomparable grace and charm here. A feeling of happy intoxication bathes the whole countryside, where the smile of flowers escorts the passer-by.

> " Here the fields are tinted with myriad hues,
>   Here the young vine clings to the slender elm,
>   Here the cool shade of gently-moving leaves . . ."

Reality is a little different.

*After the hard preparatory work of the winter months, the Land Army girls enjoy making a haystack in the summer sunshine.*

Agricultural work has certainly very little of the mysterious about it, but it is work which demands a great deal of judgment and a great store of experience. The countryman must in turn be zoologist, botanist, biologist, chemist, meteorologist and even a mechanic. He has no control over cold or rain, thunder or storms, or drought.

Here is a farm with 125,000 fruit trees. They have to be pruned. Which branch should be cut? Or should it be split? When should it be done? How many times must the arms be lifted to pick the fruit? Millions of times!

Nature does not reveal her secrets to impatient people. Here is another farm. There are 10,000 birds here. For us, the townspeople, one pullet looks much like another. Yet the awkward movements of this one disclose a hidden tumour; another has a contagious disease which may well affect the whole poultry run.

50,000 tomato plants. To "nip" tomatoes appears to be the simplest operation in the world. Have you ever tried systematically to correct the prodigality of nature?

All this work, in which personal intuition plays such a big part, is done by the land girls. They manage it all, to the great astonishment of their employers, who received them at the beginning with a certain amount of scepticism.

They do many other jobs too, and many harder ones. They thresh the corn by machine. They work the cutting, binding and threshing machines. They drive the tractors, which draw heavy, five-pronged ploughs; the furrows have to be straight, but great mounds of earth slyly turn the machine off its course. They carry heavy trusses of fodder in great armfuls. They saw up the trees and steep them in sulphate. They handle lead acetate and nicotine. They make careful selection of the potatoes. They keep watch over the incubators, from which thousands of little chicks will swarm, and these will later supply the tables of the city dwellers, who know nothing of the hard work of the fields. With sure, unhesitating movements they place the aluminium identity discs between the wing bones of the little chicks, without causing them a single squeak of pain.

If, in this heroic isle, besieged now for three years, we are not going hungry, this is due in no small part to these happy land girls.

*Twelve girls are employed on the London County Council Horton, Surrey farm, and are making a great success of their work. Here are some of the girls giving a 2-weeks-old lamb a meal from a feeding bottle.*

# WISE

## and foolish virgins

WHAT DO THESE women think about as they tackle their jobs ?

People who are not familiar with the average worker are too ready to imagine that the pay packet is their main thought. This is quite wrong. During the first three months of the war, British employers carried out an inquiry among their staffs, covering tens of thousands of individuals. It was an endeavour to trace causes of worry or discontent among work-people. The result was most surprising; the black-out was the most frequent cause of a somewhat troubled state of mind. The question of pay, if my memory is correct, held sixth or seventh place among the reasons for anxiety. The food question, difficulties of transport, conditions of work and also the reasons and causes of the war and preparation for the future came

A little Yorkshire village claims to be the only one to have an "All Girls" fire squad. Betty Banks, a 22-year-old railway clerk, started it and the squad call themselves the Women's Voluntary Fire Service.

The "Ack-Ack" girls who go into action against night raiders. Here are some of the girls in the London Area at work on their height-finder on a gun site. Theirs is dangerous and responsible work.

*In the Regional control room at a London Fire Station, Fireman Manuel is shown locating on the mobilization board, while W.N.F.S keep in touch with sub-stations.*

well before the question of remuneration, which is so often held to be the strongest motive-power for mankind.

I have been able to prove by personal contact and questions how true are these observations, collated during the first three months of the war. As far as wages are concerned, exceptional cases are often cited which might lead people to believe that these were reaching astronomical figures. This too is quite wrong. It is true, however, that a number of women and young people who had not been earning money before, are doing so now.

I happened one day, during an air raid alert, to be in a factory canteen. Between six and seven hundred women had just finished their meal. A talkie apparatus was showing films of current events and cartoons on a screen decorated at the top with British, American and Soviet flags. There was not the slightest trace of emotion. The audience was far more interested in Walt Disney's animated figures than in the sirens. Only the spotters left the room to go up on the roofs and order the factory to be cleared should the danger become imminent—and this would take only two minutes to do.

Such sang-froid is clearly a special characteristic of the British race.

But I noticed another thing; the woman who works is constantly on the defensive against any suggestion of an ant-like existence. She tries by every possible means to prevent her own personality becoming flattened by the compressor roller, shaping mass-production models in manufacture and in life.

The women in the factories have well-cared-for hands and hair and they wear, whenever possible, pretty shoes. They have not given up their necklaces nor their bracelets nor their lipsticks. Most of them wear the regimental badges of their husbands, sons or fiances

*While her men colleagues fit up a trailer pump, an N.F.S. girl picks her way through the debris. Women are now co-operating with the men in fire-fighting.*

on their overalls. Some of them even wear several . . . "Safety in numbers." The ways of the feminine heart are impenetrable.

Strict and testy moralists would rail against such coquetry. Personally, I am grateful to these women for such innocent and gallant retaliation to the ugliness of war.

And when in a canteen for women making war-weapons I see a piano, a gramophone or a radio set, I am glad that these young music-lovers are not deprived of their sharps and flats. After all, the Blues, the Charleston and Tangos are fortunately not as yet among the things which Lord Woolton has rationed. When questioned about the future, or about their personal plans, they show two strongly-opposed sets of ideas. Some, especially those subjected to the very strict military discipline of camp life, are homesick for their dishes, their mending and their cradles. Others, however, those in the factories—and they are by far the most numerous— wish to continue along the course they have chosen.

Where then are the wise and the foolish virgins? I, for one, would not like to have to say.

Yet these young women are not only concerned with their own personal fate, which would be reasonable enough, but are also anxious about the future of their country and that of the world. If I had to summarise in a word the predominant state of mind among them, I should say—"Impatient confidence." They know that we will win the war. They are the more certain of this because they are manufacturing the instruments of our victory, but they get impatient because it does not come quickly enough. And this impatience increases with the growing quantity of war material they are producing.

The feminine element, far more than the male, has undergone a far-reaching professional change in Great Britain. If the women wish to remain in the factories after the war, these factories will first have to transform their present production into one suited to peacetime. But that will not be enough. They will also have to find outlets for the stocks which will mount at an incredible rate, for the tools have reached gigantic proportions.

In this connection, I have found the industrialists far more

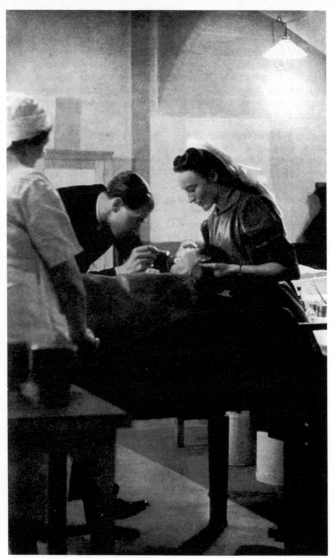

*All over the country members of the Civil Nursing Reserve are doing valuable work in shelters, rest centres, hospitals.*

optimistic than the workers. The manager of one of the firms which had previously been manufacturing the luxurious sleeper restaurant-cars that make people begin to dream as they see them glide lightly and rapidly over the rails of the continental network, told me that it had only taken him 60 days, from the production in the drawing-office of the plans to the completion in the factory of the tank engines which he is now making. I asked him how long it would take him to reverse the change-over. With the full agreement of the technical experts standing nearby, he told me—"Just one week." This optimism is not an isolated case, it is general.

An experienced woman worker, when questioned about the possibility of outlets for goods after the signature of the Armistice, told me that the destruction caused by the War would create a considerable demand. Although I agreed with her, I nevertheless raised the objection that somebody would have to pay for these needs. She replied that the United States had applied the procedure inscribed in the Lease-Lend Act to war deliveries. What can be done for the war, she said, should be done for the peace. There is only one way, she told me—and she spoke with strong feeling—to give the people a reasonably good standard of living and an increased purchasing power, so that they can have thermos flasks, fountain pens, shoes, ploughs, cars, radio sets, etc.

It is also clearly and generally understood that the world-reconstruction of to-morrow cannot be achieved without a profound economic and social transformation, requiring a radical reduction of hours of work, the suppression of Customs' barriers, the organisation of a stable currency, the reform of international credit, etc.

Women can see a new regime developing as they watch. Through their participation in factory and production committees, and through the ever-increasing control exercised by the community on the methods of production and trade, they can see the system of private ownership changing before their eyes. New juridical forms are appearing in social relations between people. The profit motive is fast losing the important place it had as an incitement to work.

Private interests, in countries such as England, are giving way

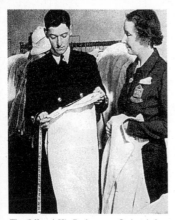

*The Officers' Kit Replacement Society is kept busy supplying clothes of every description to officers who have lost their outfits through enemy action. A young New Zealander, attached to the Fleet Air Arm, receives tropical kit from Mrs. Matthews, of the W.V.S.*

*Mrs. Mary Couchman is a 24-year-old warden in a small Kentish town. This picture was taken during an actual raid, when this brave woman crouched over three frightened children caught in the street, to protect them from bomb splinters with her own body.*

more and more to those of the community. There is no longer room for privileges and class interests. The latter are certainly opposed to this tendency towards a form of society which must register the death certificate of its predecessor. There is, however, a growing movement towards production for the satisfaction of definite needs, and not only for profit.

The workers, imbued with a longing and love for democracy, feel that the trade unions to which they belong are playing a decisive and historic role in this evolution.

From the description which I have just given, one might think that Great Britain will soon have as idle drones, only a few shivering, sickly or undeveloped males. We have not quite reached that point yet, but it would be a grave mistake to believe that women will willingly and spontaneously disappear from the field of production and commerce, in which they have been compelled to take a place.

More and more they will play the role which they deserve, and they will play it well. Great Britain, defending her freedom, has contracted an immense debt of gratitude to the women. And so have we all.

*A Women's Royal Naval Service dispatch rider carries an urgent message to an Officer of a destroyer, which has just returned to port after patrol duties*